DRAWING PROMPTS

365 FUN AND WACKY DRAWING PROMPTS

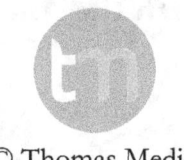

© Thomas Media

Founded in 2017, Thomas Media is a publisher of gift books, creative books, innovative journals, cards, notepads and stationery. Thomas Media publishes over 50 books and ancillary products per year.

© Thomas Media
Visit us at Thomasmedia.ie

ISBN: 9798694085724

Printed: United States

As a small company, we rely on your reviews to keep costs low for our customers and improve our products. Please spare a moment rate or review this book on Amazon and share your experience with the Amazon community.

"Drawing Prompts" © Thomas Media Limited 2020. All rights reserved. No part of this kit shall be reproduced, stored in a retrieval system, or transmitted by any means – electronic, mechanical, photocopying, recording, or otherwise – without written permission from the publisher.

A Fish Teasing a Fisherman

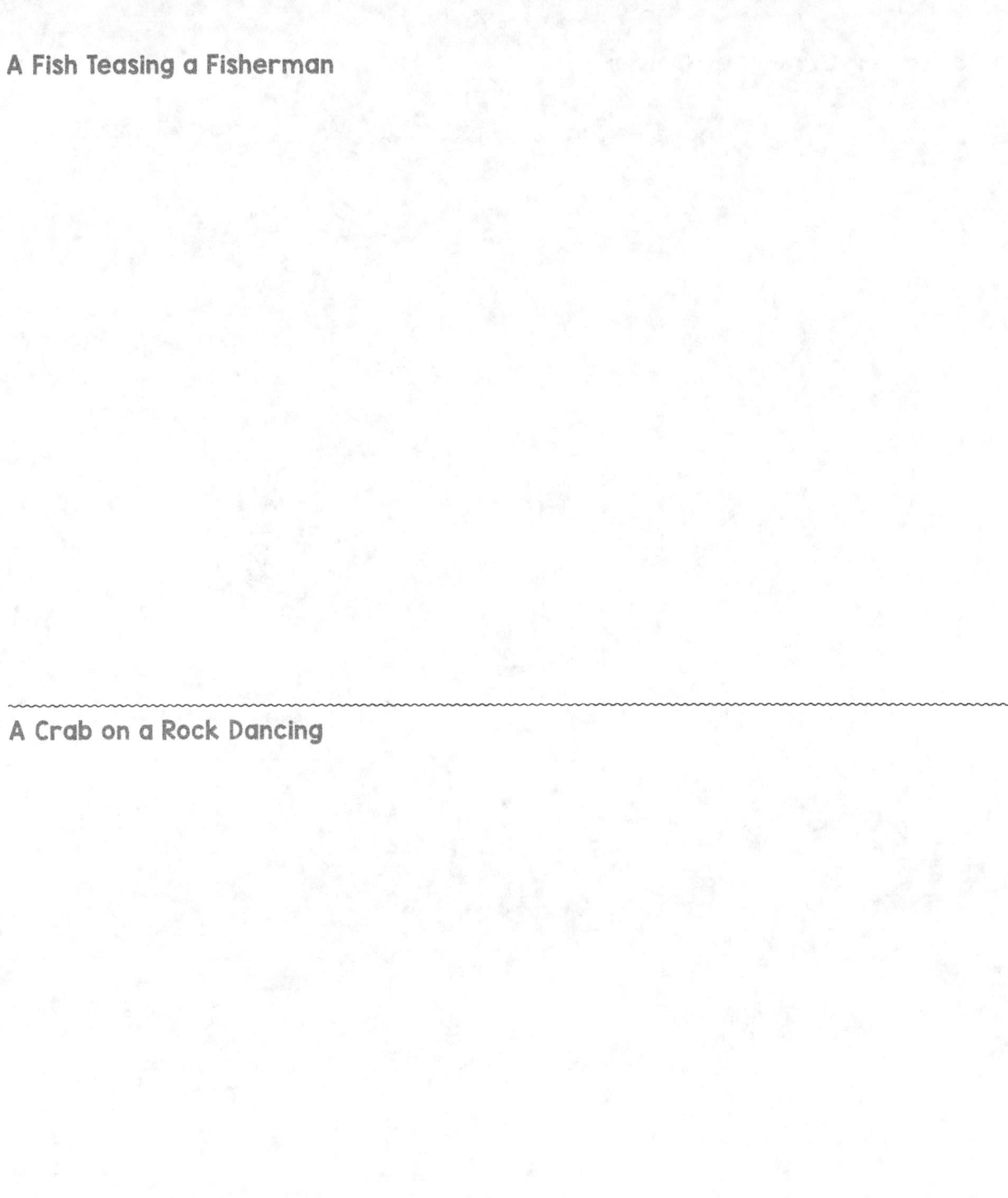

A Crab on a Rock Dancing

A Car Driving at Night by Clowns

A Measuring Tape for Sweets

Exploding Raindrops Falling in a Puddle

A Head Torch that Creates Darkness

Face Cream that Grows Hair

A Set of Talking Car Keys

A Collection of Old Magazines Talking

An Instant Camera Capturing Someone's Thoughts

A Tipsy Wine Rack

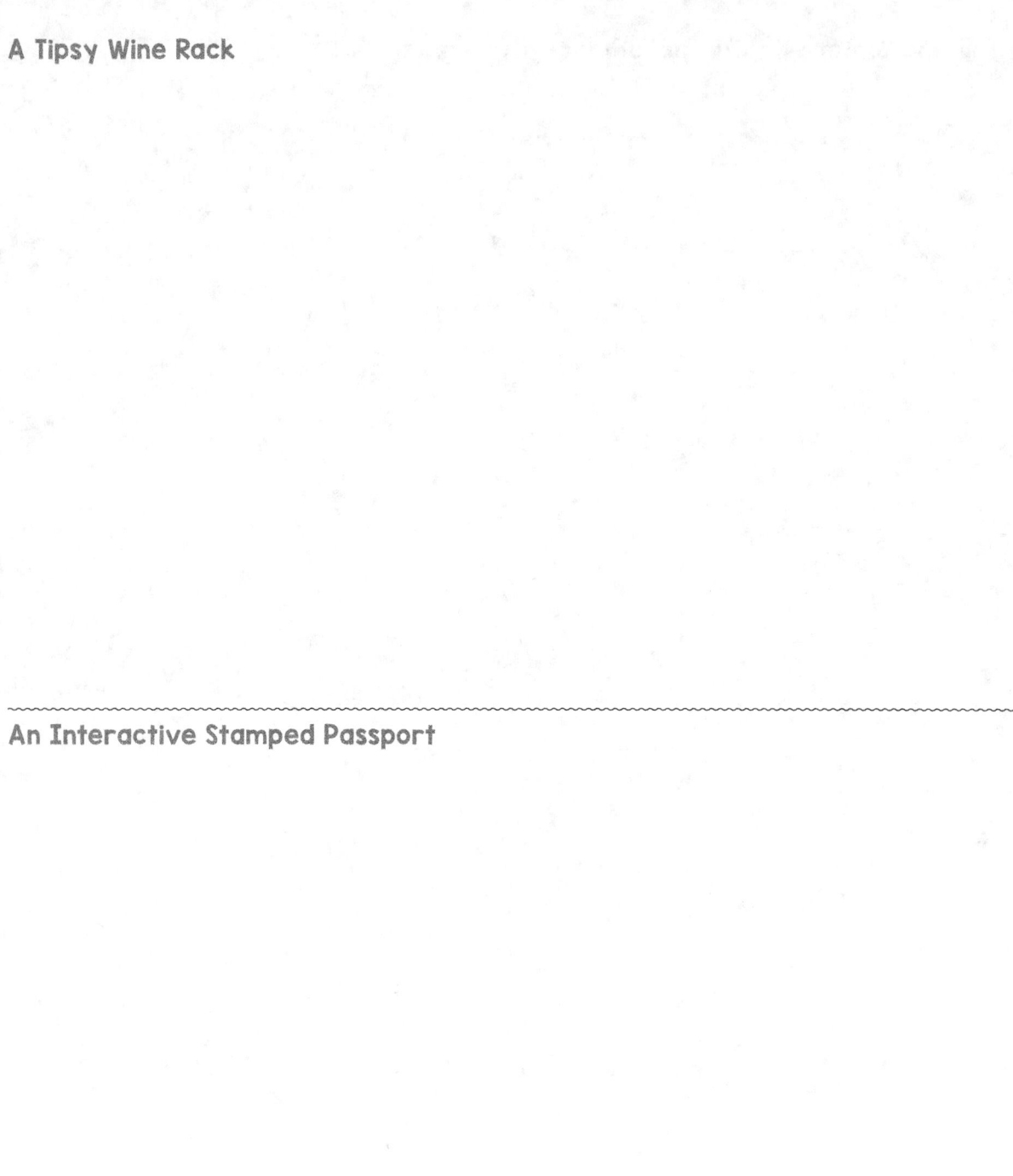

An Interactive Stamped Passport

An Old Storefront Made from Candy

Hairspray - Freeze Spray

A Photographer Shoots with Blurred Vision

A Fishing Bag with Live Fish

~~~~~~
An Old World War Airplane Gets Angry

A Newspaper

A Hen

A Kite

A Wine Opener

Let's Face It - Draw the Above Items with Faces.

Three Pigs Playing Poker

Old Boots Dancing

A Penguin and a Navigation Chart

A Walled Picture Comes to Life

A Priest on a Surfboard

A Wine Bottle and Glass Cosying Up Together

A Wire Cable Tossing Birds into the Air

A Hamburger Speaks Their Mind

A Rubber Duck Enjoying the Bath Tub

A Coke Bottle Exploding

A Lighthouse Sprays Light Across the Sea

A Pencil Sharpener	An Cooking Apron
A Paint Brush	A Stop Sign

Let's Body It - Draw the Above Items with a Body.

Dancing Shoes Stand Off

A Ladybird Popping Colored Spots

A Butterfly Crashing into a Flower

A Spiders Web

~~~~~~
A Boat Wreck in an Ocean Cave

An Evil Ride on Lawnmower

A Magic Gate

A Radio Station Pumping out Silence

Expressions After a Scary Elevator Ride

A Vampire Party

A Rain Cloud that Follows You

A Cupcake Winking at You

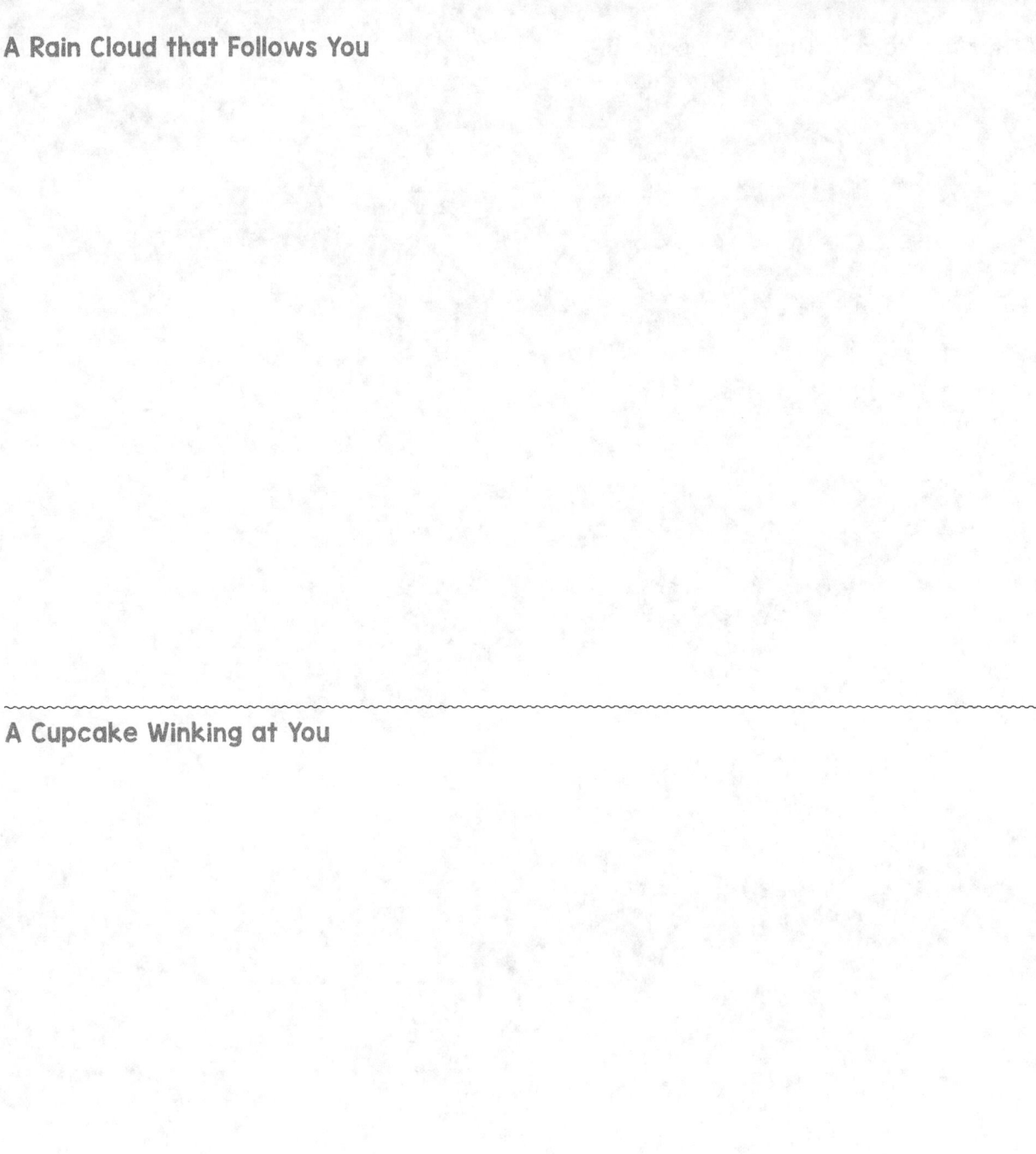

A Hot Air Balloon That Only Goes UP

A Steak Sizzling on a Pan

An Exhausted Wind Gauge

~~~~~~

How You Feel Right Now

A Bunch of Old Tomatoes

A Talking Apple Pie

Lipstick	A Fancy Hat
An Apron	**Old Spectacles**

Let's Woman It - Draw the Above Items Including the Face of a Woman

A Flexible Loyalty Card

A Mean Wallet

A Concert Playing Without People

A Window Display Comes Alive

A Box of Self Exploding Matches

A Scary Owl Looks You Up and Down

An Enchanted Forest

A Stereo Comes to Life

A Reflection in the Water

Something You See Right Now

An Street of Umbrellas

Snowfall with Parachutes

A Sneaky Pair of Slippers

A Rude Digital Display

A Jacuzzi Bubbles

A Bird Crash Lands

A Pirate Climbs the Ships Mast

A Joker Playing Card

The Winning Lotto Ticket

A Crying Postcard

The Face of a Man Who's Just Tasted Something Disgusting

A Common Sense Dispenser

A Biting Vending Machine

A Big Spooky Old House

A Statue of You

A Vampire Sleeping in Your Closet

One Wheel Bicycles in Amsterdam

A Grandfather Shirt	A Hammer
A Hairstyle	**Drinking Coffee**

Let's Man It - Draw the Above Items Including the Face of a Man

A Joke You Heard

An Idea You Have

A Crazy Invention to Change the World

A Mysterious Food Market With Eyes Everywhere

A Dog Chasing a Cat

Cooking Utensils with Food

A Cat Hiding from a Dog

A Monster Eating Breakfast at Your Table

An Giant Insect in Your Backyard

A Man in an Ice Bath

A Fairy Fortress

A Ghost Patrols the House

A Mysterious Shadow

ns in the Mall

A Packet of Jelly's	A Christmas Stocking
An Elf Lover	A Mustache

Let's Elf It - Draw the Above Items Including an Elf

A Lumberjack Stuck Up a Tree

A Tree Chasing a Chainsaw in the Woods

A Rabbit in a Hat

A Kissing Booth

A Caveman Singing Opera

A Bowl of Lemons Speaking French

A Rainbow Dripping Colors

Tattoo Art Comes Alive

A Venus Fly Trap

An Octopus - What does he do?

A Robot at the Store Checkout

An Aileen Drinking Coffee

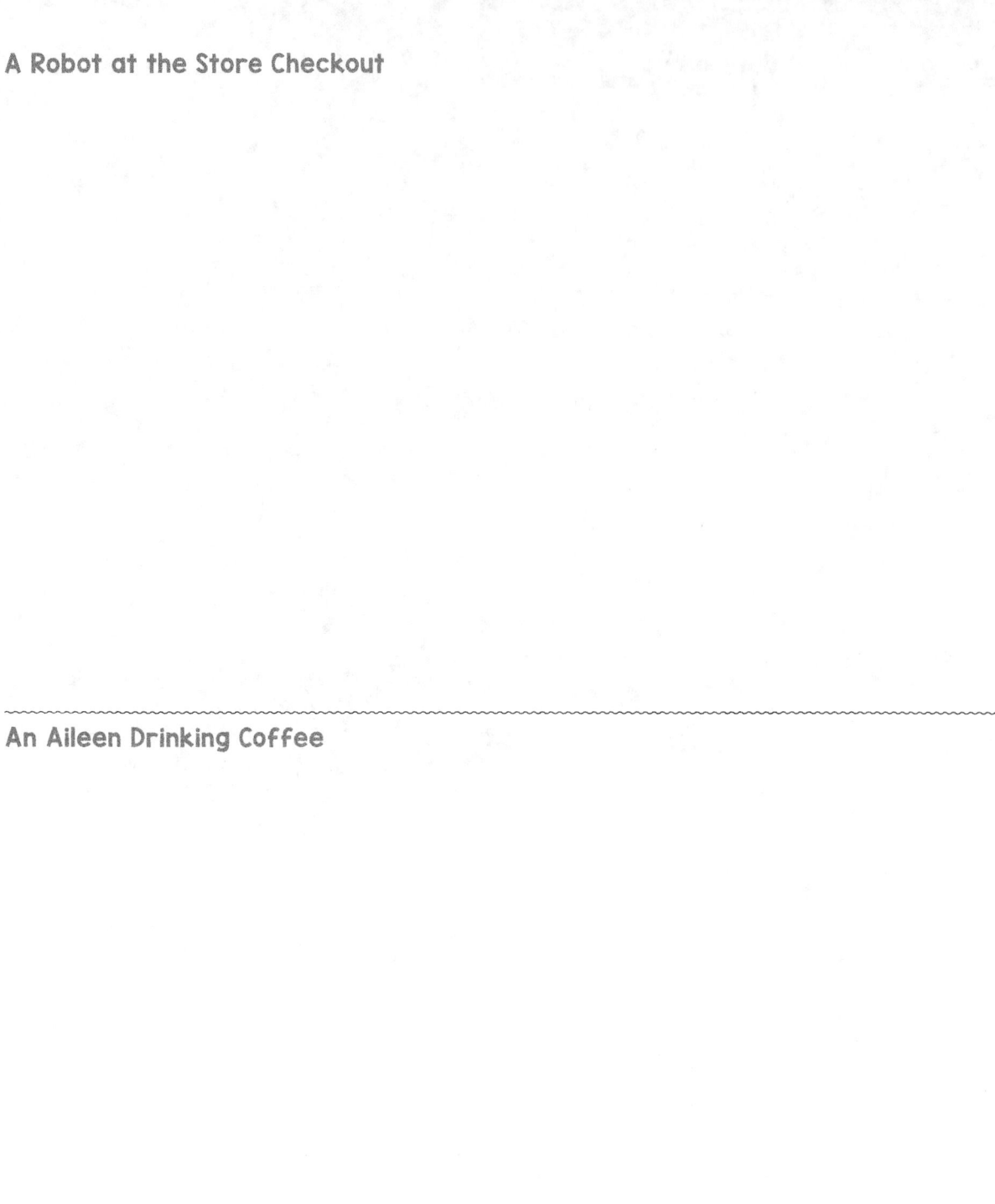

An Elegant Lady at Lunch

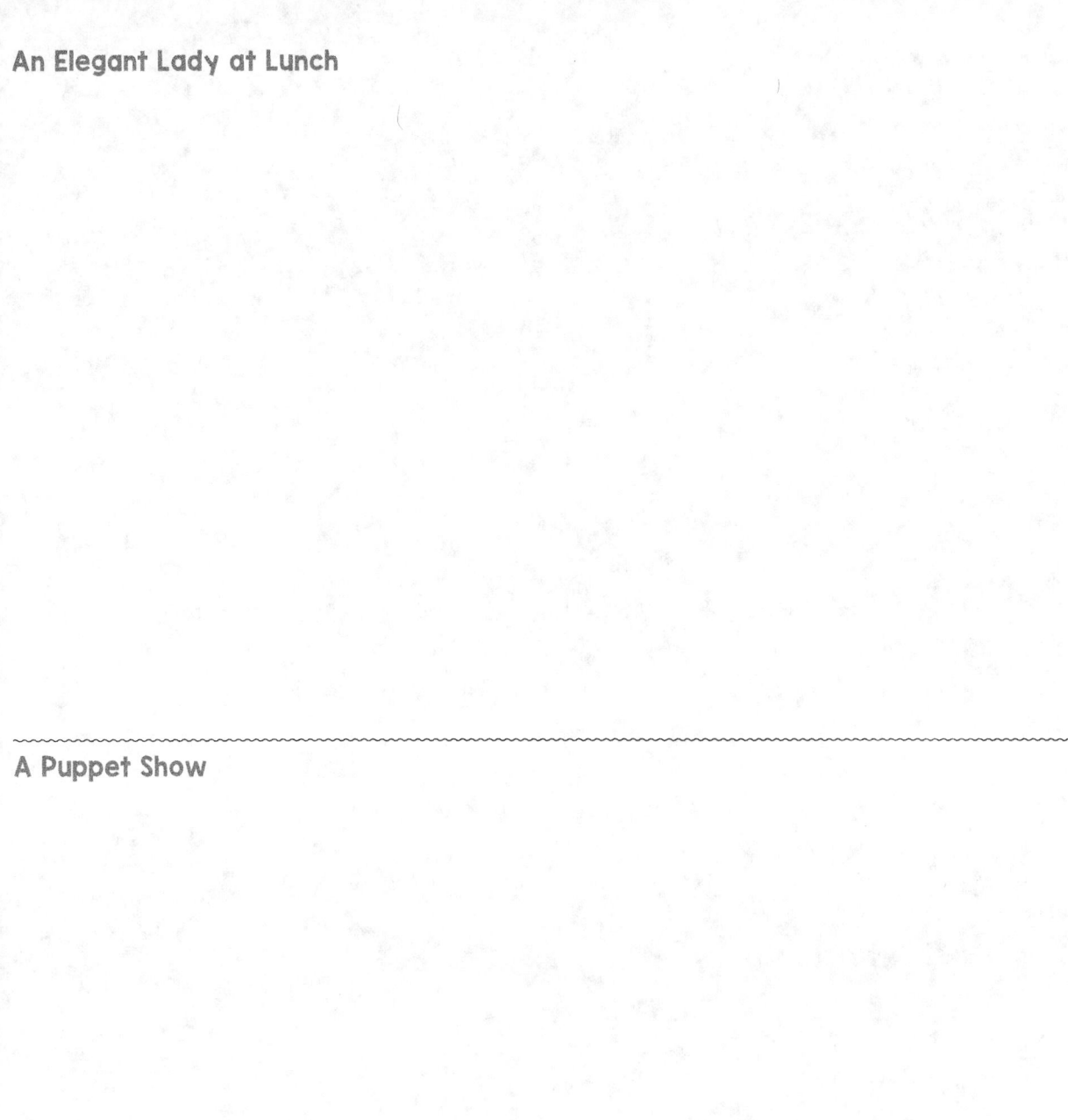

A Puppet Show

A Ballerina's Gym Bag

A Mad Scientist

A Scientific Experiment

A Mexican Pineapple Smoking

A Beach Scene where the Sand is Ice Cream

An Axe Crazed Cat Fights Back

3 Witches Chanting a Spell

A Bear Market

A Hotdog with Lips

Music in the Air

A Banana Skin Slip

Your Old Teacher has Secret Tentacles

A Kangaroo Holding a Gun

Your Worst Enemy

Something You See Right Now

Pinocchio's Nose	US Flag
A Voting Card	A Weapon of Choice

Let's Trump It - Draw the Above Items Including the Face of Donald Trump

A Vegetable Patch Fighting

The Spooky Shed at the Bottom of the Garden

A Dancing Toaster

A Wizard Performing a Spell

An Artist Drawing a Portrait

Converse Sneakers

A Spaceship Lands in Your School/Office

A Fictional Candy Bar

An Astronauts Floating in Space

People Stranded on Desert Island

Frankenstein in an Old Telephone Booth

A Crowns	A Zoo Keeper
A Bunch of Bananas	A Cage

Let's Zoo It - Draw the Above Items Including Animals from the Zoo

Dinosaurs Chasing People in a Park

Lions in a Cage

An Ambulance Roaring Through the City

Something You See Right Now

A Musical Instrument Played by a Seal

A Music Sound Sheet Comes Alive

A Spotty Teenager

Snow White's New Dwarves (Pushy? Hypochondriac? Brainless? Ruthless? Raggedy?)

Acrobats in a Circus

Clowns on a Train

People Working in an Office

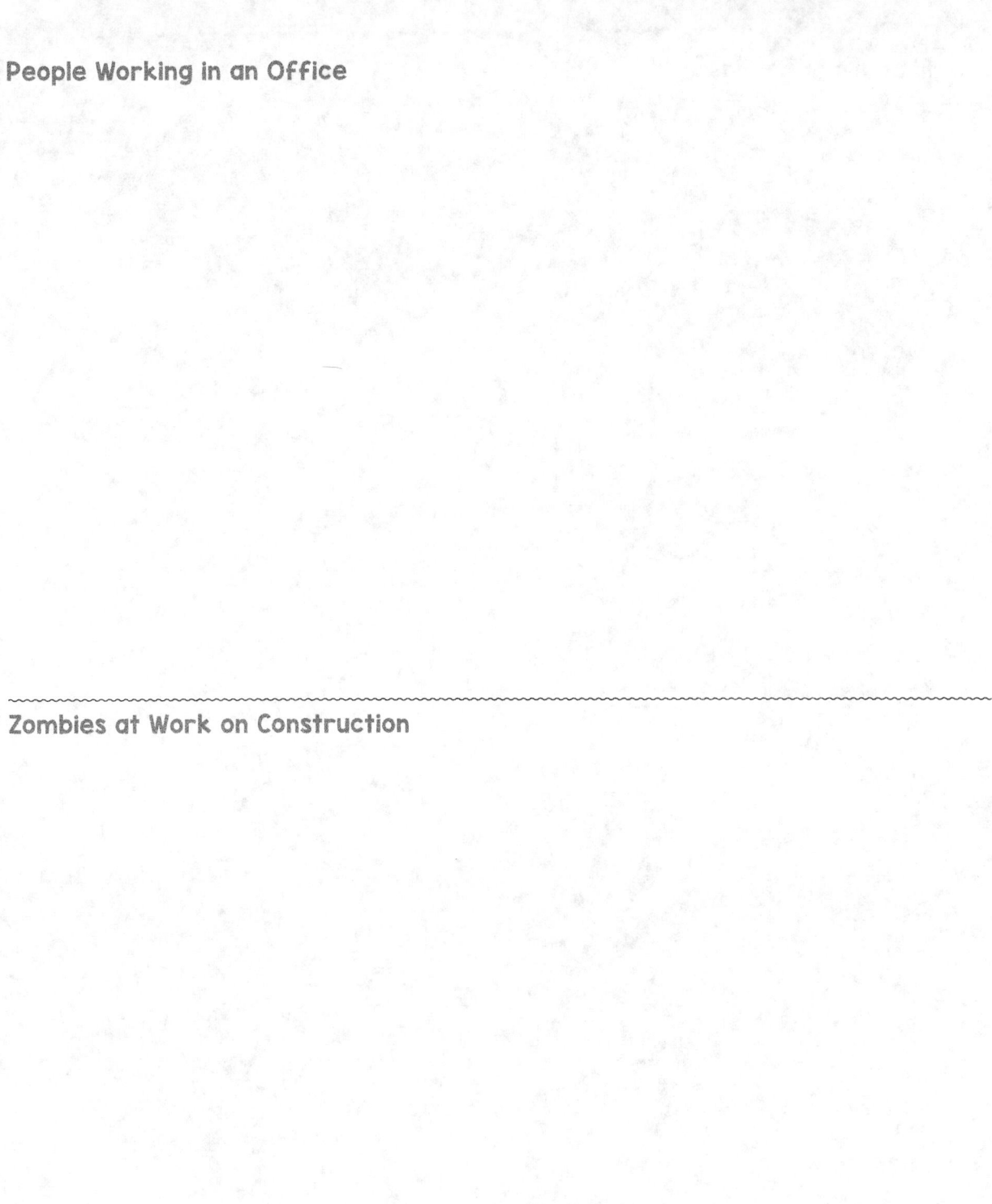

Zombies at Work on Construction

An Animal Wearing Glasses

Monsters on a Roller Coaster

A Presidential Mascot

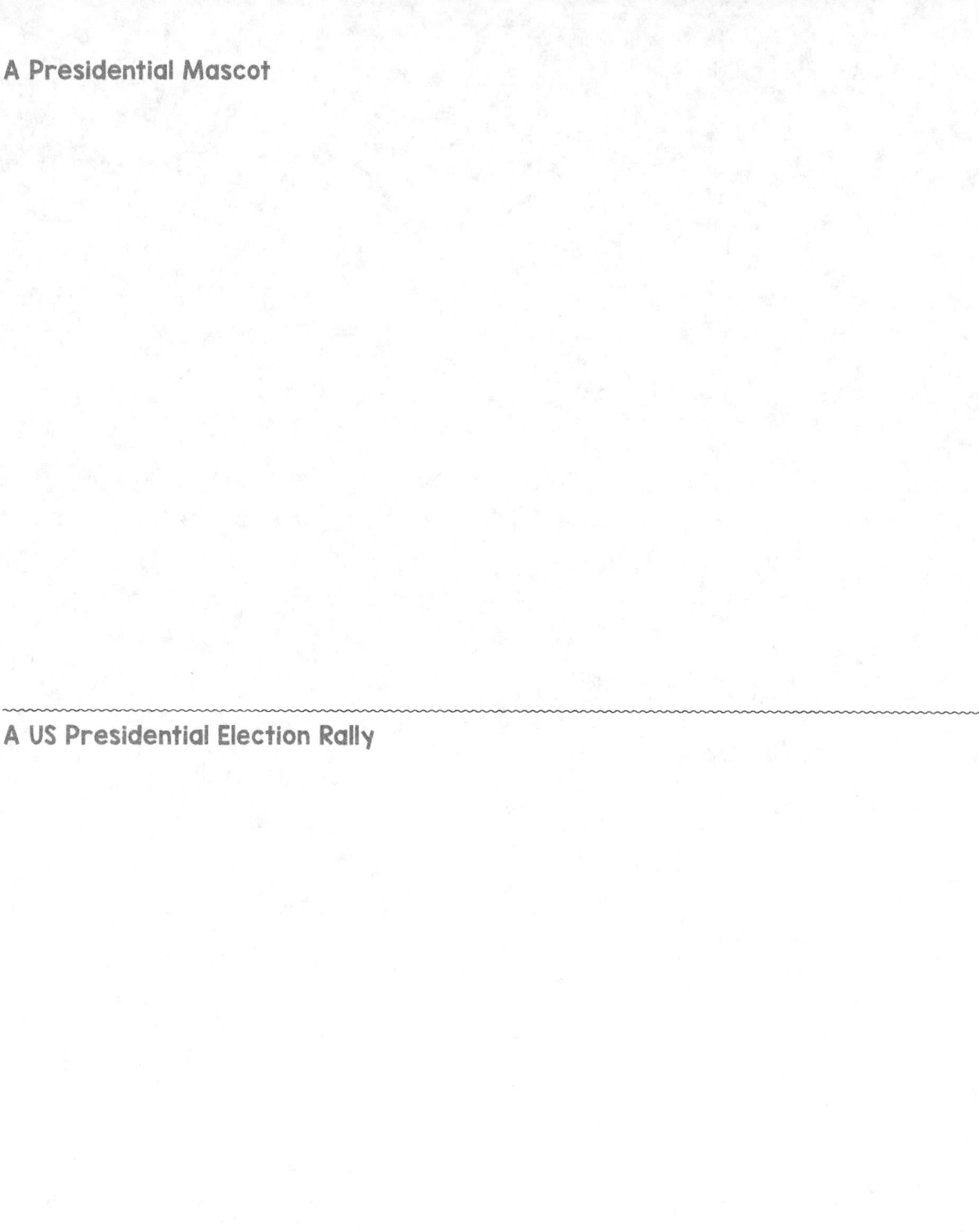

A US Presidential Election Rally

A Deserted Cargo Ship

A Two Heaed Alien

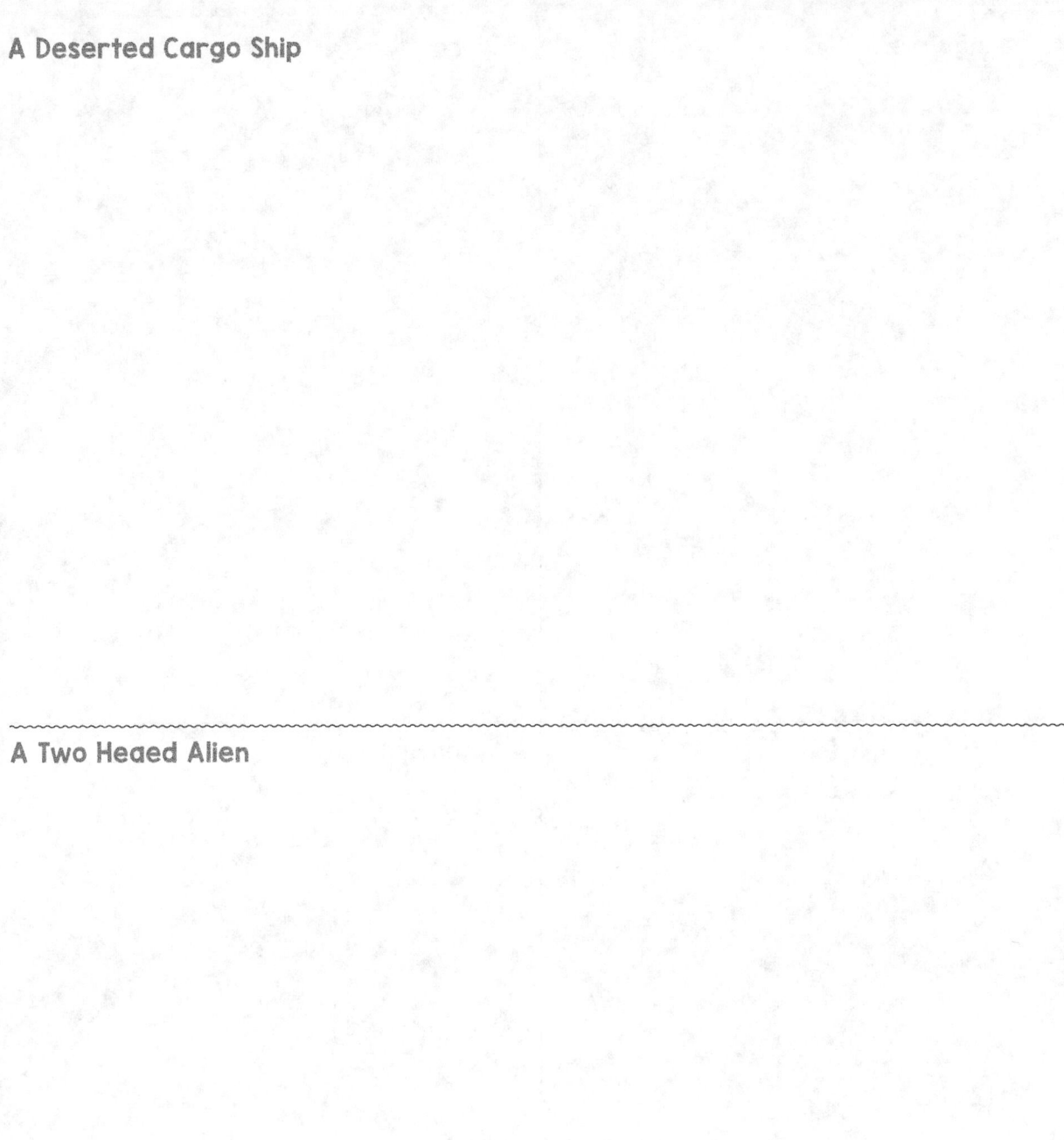

A Fishing Pole	A Worm
A Market	A Campfire

Let's Fish It - Draw the Above Items Including Fish Elements

Drunk Astronauts in Space

~~~~~~

The Cow Jumping Over the Moon

A Mouse and Cheese Trap

A Snowman Gets Kidnapped

Willy Wonka Chocolate Factory

A Baby with a Fabulous Mustache

An Animal Kissing Booth

A Punk Rocking Street Musician

A Snail Dinner

A Cavewoman Tantrum

Something You See Right Now

A Demon Under the Bed

A Game Show Host

A Turtle Stealing Jewels

The Mona Lisa Stare of Death

A K9 Police Dog Attacks

A Policeman on Horseback

Novelty Socks

A Lobster with Napkin, Knife and Fork is Ready for Dinner

Your Family are Monsters

A Bartender Serving Bloody Cocktails

A Spotted Mushroom Wins the Oscars

Usain Bolt Winning the 100m

A Shopping Cart Throws Out Food It Doesn't Like

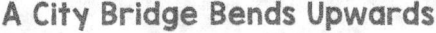
A City Bridge Bends Upwards

Snowmen Playing Soccer

Guitar Hero

A Kiss	A Bite
Standing Still	**Up Close and Personal**

Let's Zombie It - Draw the Above Items Including Zombies

Three Horses Wrapped in Blankets

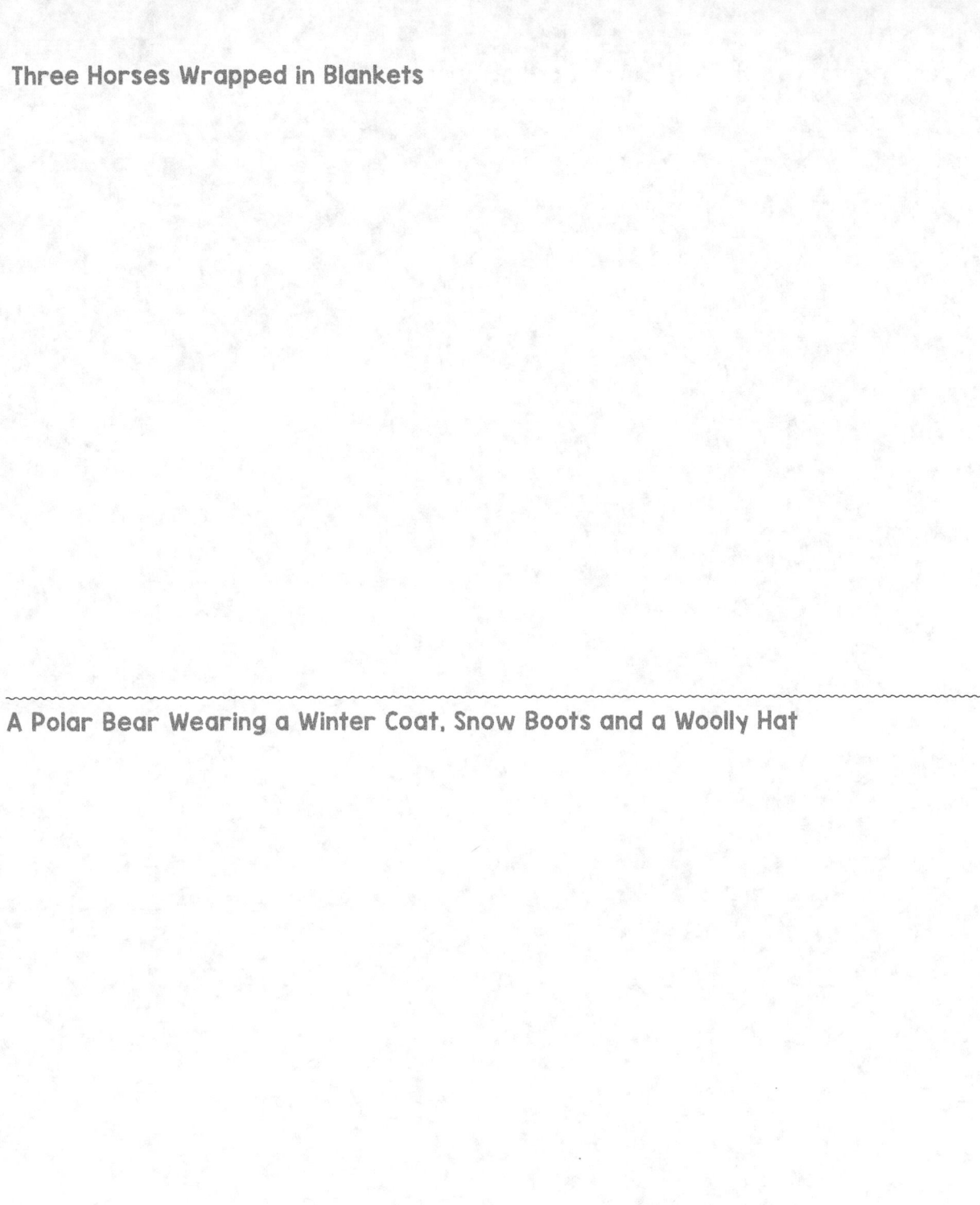

A Polar Bear Wearing a Winter Coat, Snow Boots and a Woolly Hat

A Duck Fights with the Starbucks Cashier over Coffee

Coffee Cup with Eyes and Ears

A Dirty Old Garbage Bin

A Loving Rocking Horse

A Skeleton Key

An X-Ray Pair of Binoculars

A Self Portrait

Rome and Roman Soldiers

A Squirrel at a Nut Party

A Raincoat with Magic Shield

A Man in Chains

A Penguin Dancing

A Tree House	A Yo-yo
A Bucket and Spade	**A Rain Jacket**

Let's Mouse It - Draw the Above Items Including Mice

A Dartboard that Doesn't Like Darts

Viking Archery Practice

A Car Dashboard that Tells You What It Thinks

A Kite Flying in the Park Dodging Birds

A Waterfall in Summer Filled with Swimming Monkeys

An Abandoned Building

A Leprechaun Warehouse by the Docks

A Mermaid Party

A Wooden Fence Along a Cliff Edge

Strangers in the Coffee Shop

A Chocolate Maze

A Secret Tunnel

A Buildings Emergency Staircase

Something You See Right Now

An Entrance	**A Gold Tooth**
A Piece of Jewelry	**A Hat**

Let's Pimp It - Draw the Above Items Including Pimps

A Smiling Pumpkin

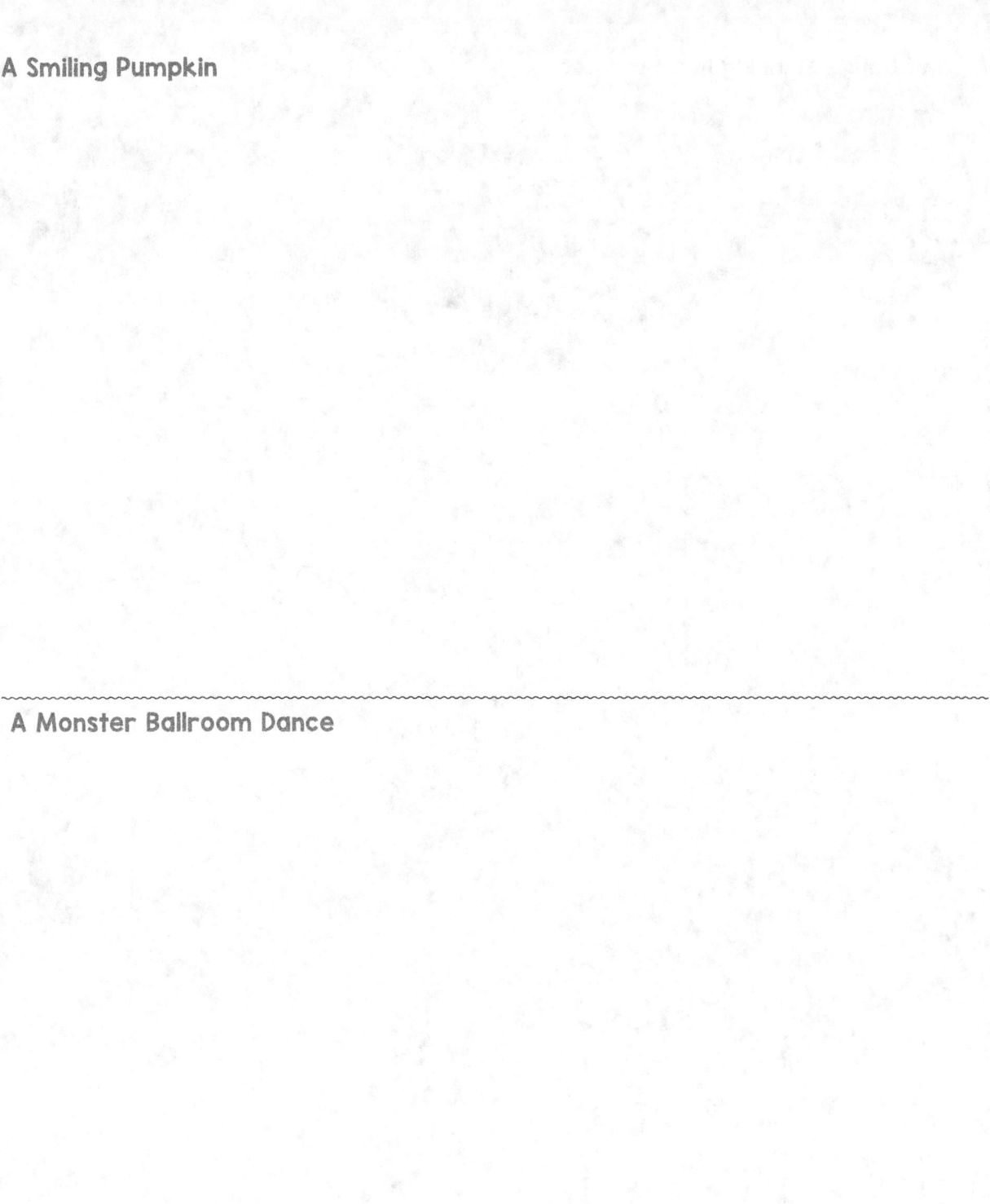

A Monster Ballroom Dance

A Wind Gauge Spinning in a Hurricane

A Robot Eating Cereal

A Suspicious Milkshake

A Ceiling Fan with a Cat Grabbing On

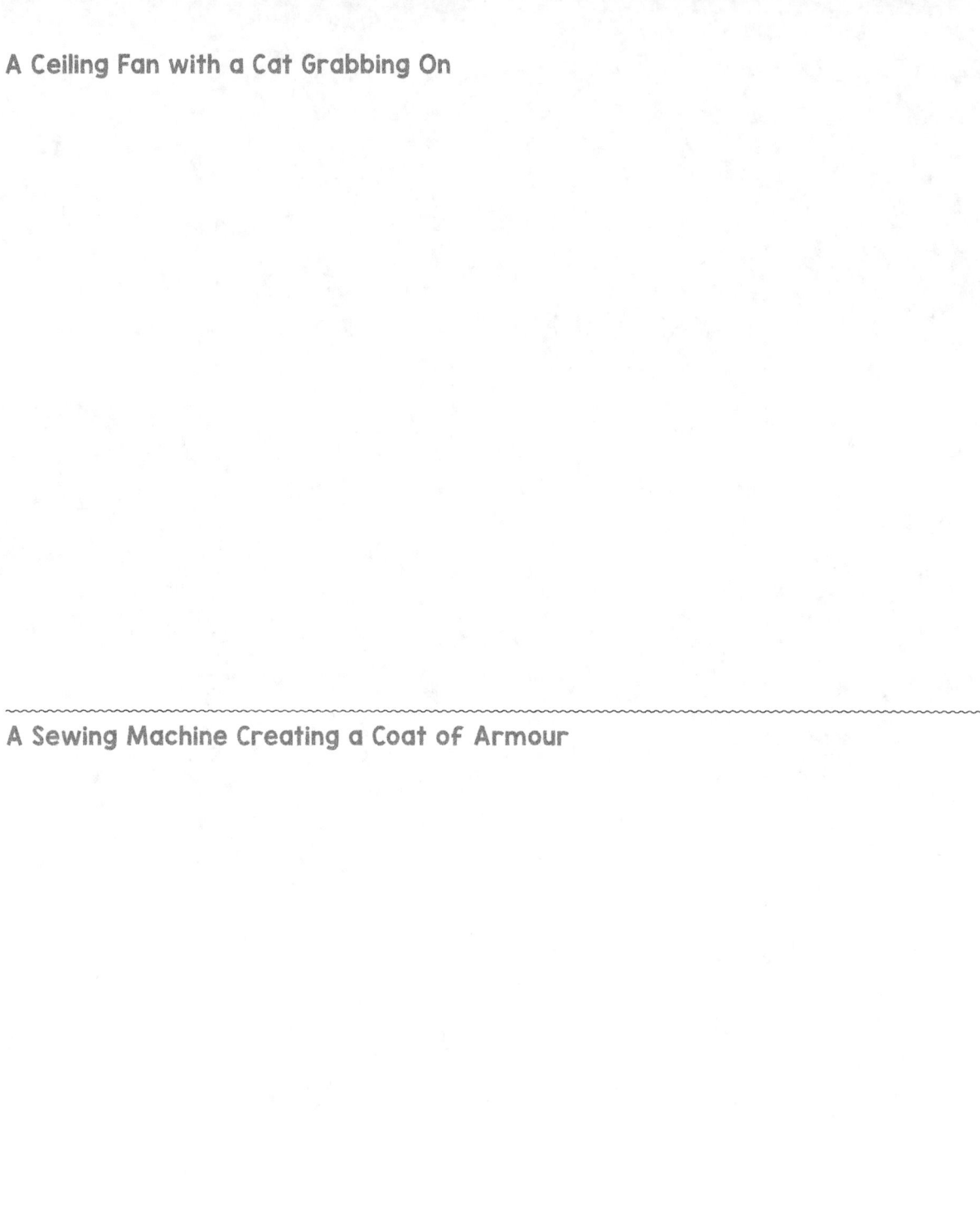

A Sewing Machine Creating a Coat of Armour

Logs Stacked by the Fire Flare Up

A Baby Circus Ringmaster

A Clock Store Comes to Life

Elephants on a Spiralling Mountain Road

Electric Coffee Beans in a Bag

A Time Traveller from the Past

Something You See Right Now

Game Over	Not Nice
Time	Loser

Let's Bully It - Draw the Above Items Including a Bully

A Hockey Player Collides

A Baseball Player Trips

A Basketball Player Soars

A Personalized Birthday Cake

Party Balloons Popping

A Mechanics Toolbox Frozen in Ice

A Suspect in a Crime

A Clever Fox

A Dessert Defends Itself

A Dog House Traps the Invading Cat

A Palm Tree by the Beach

The Queen of England Gets Rowdy

One Eyed Monster

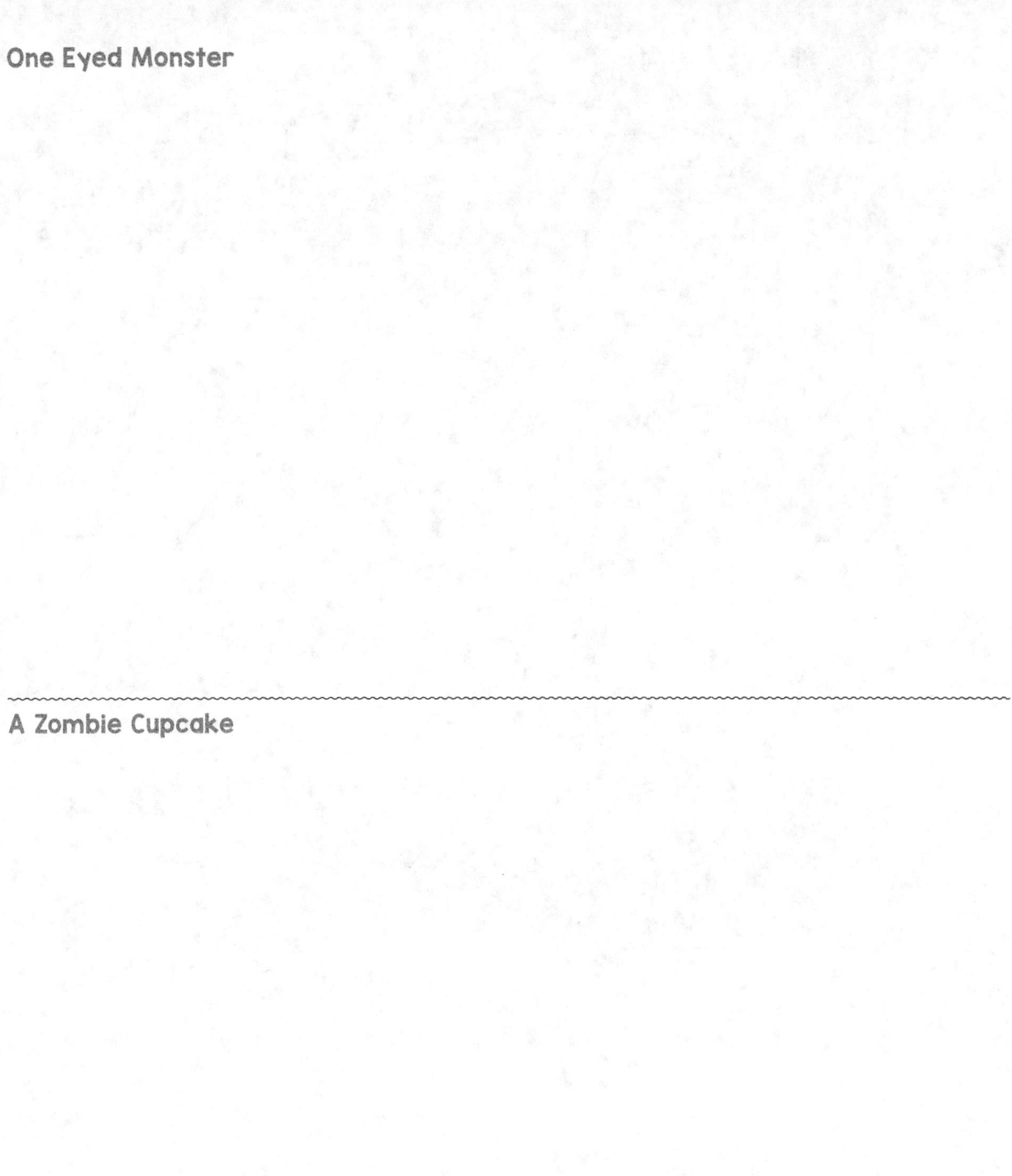

A Zombie Cupcake

A Street Parade Full of Insects

A Waitress in a Diner

A Firefighter Afraid of Fire

A Tired Human Eye

A Train Tunnel Approaches

Earrings on a Rich Lady

A Swing in the Backyard

A Fishing Rod Bends

A Fishing Boat Captain

Inside an Ambulance with Dog Medics

A Hammock	A Foot Massage
A Mask	Feet Up

Let's Relax It - Draw the Above Items Including an Element of Relaxation

A Mouse Tailor Measures You for a Suit

The Gates to a Graceland

A Combination Lock

A Vintage Car with Melons for Wheels

A Car Broken Down Engulfed in Smoke

A Strawberry Gives You a Pep Talk

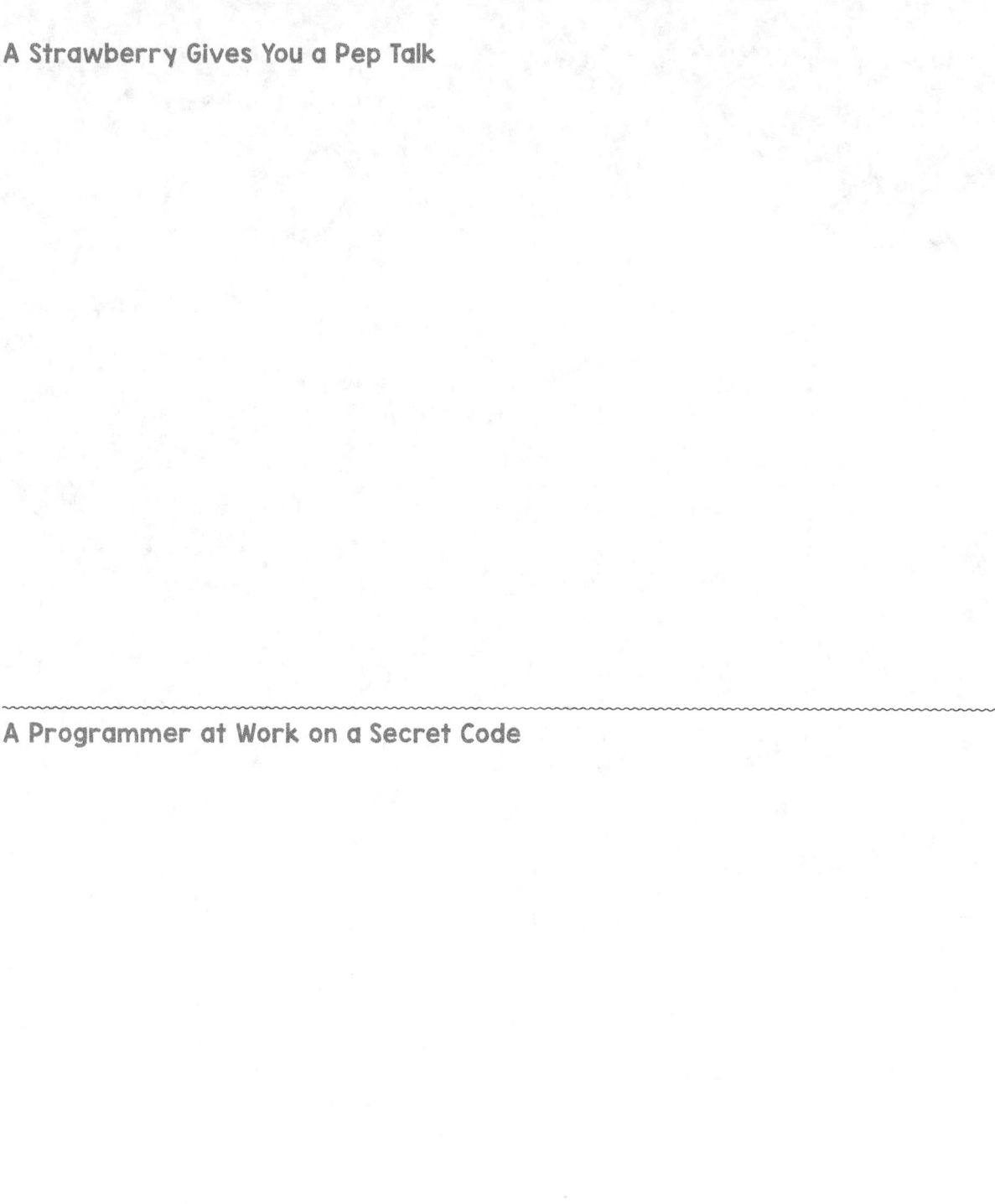

A Programmer at Work on a Secret Code

A Cold Starry Night Sky

Camping on a Glacier with A Polar Bear

An Escalator in a Shopping Mall in Reverse

A Massive Spy Telescope

A Barbers Hands

A Scarecrow Wrestles with a Giant Crow

An Opera for Babies

Blueprints for a Fun House

A Scarecrow Face

A Famous Logo Bursts

Mickey Mouse the Rapper

A Dolphin Performing

A Quarterback Catching a Hot Dog Mid Game

A Cash Register Eating Money

Shopping Bags with Legs

A Windmill with Personality

Dancing Flowers in a Garden

A Mailbox	A Horse
A Hat	**A Demon**

Let's Post It - Draw the Above Items Including an Element of Postal Services

Something I See Right Now

Monster Working in Google

Sunbathing with a Crab

A Dress Made from Banana Skinks

A Pillow of Live Ducks

A Robot Vacuum Cleaner

A Footprint in the Snow

A Gorilla Penalty Shoot Out

A Visit to the Fishmonger By Sharks

A Smurf Forest Trail

A Scary Clown on a Bicycle

A Funny Smell from the Sink

Wine and Cheese Party

A Christmas Jumper

A Notice Board

A Vintage Child and Pony Carriage

A Coconut Fight

A Pencil Case Zip Line

A Bag of Rice Explodes

A Parrot in a Cage

A Mousetrap

A Storm in a Tea Cup

The Wheel of Fortune

A Game of Roulette

| Herbs | A House |

| Farm | Vegetable Patch |

Let's Green It - Draw the Above Items Including Green Elements

Something I See Right Now

A Revolver Points Itself at You

Lobster Lovers Holding Hands on the Beach

A Robot Teacher

A Submarine Passage Way

A Broken Truck on the Road

A Train Ticket to Hogwarts

A Dog Spraying Graffiti on a Wall

A Poodle and Hairspray

A Set of Teeth Clattering

Moscow in the Snow

A Man with a Fever

A Milk Carton Delivery

A Horse at a Fence Giving Out to Passer-by's

A Grumpy Moon

A Cup and Saucer Party

A Gondola in Venice

A Killer Rodent

Napoleon Takes a Selfie

A Donut in Disguise

A Dancing Hippo Working in Starbucks

An Emergency Exit in a Wild West Salon

Sign Up to ThomasMedia.ie

Thomas Media is an independent publisher based in Dublin, Ireland. At Thomas Media, we are passionate about books and our readers. We would like to invite you to become a member of community and enjoy exclusive benefits. With already 25,000 happy customers worldwide, we promise you'll be in good company.

- Up to 50% off your next website purchases
- Access to free offers
- Birthday gifts
- Free shipping offers
- First dibs on sales
- & more...

To subscribe, simply visit our website at:

http://www.thomasmedia.ie/subscribe.html

365 Creative Series

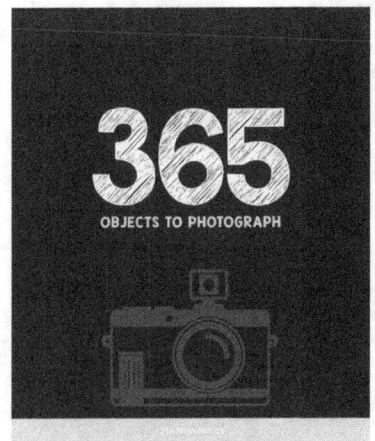
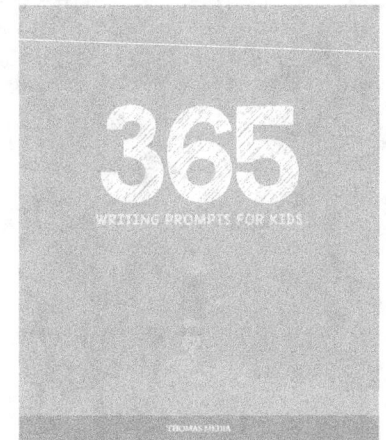
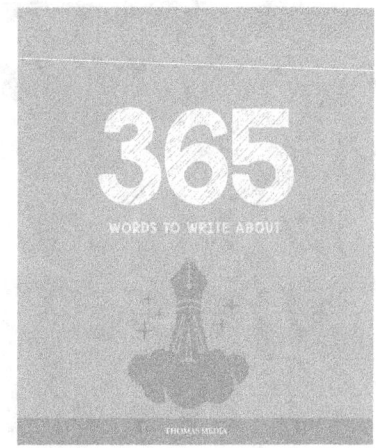
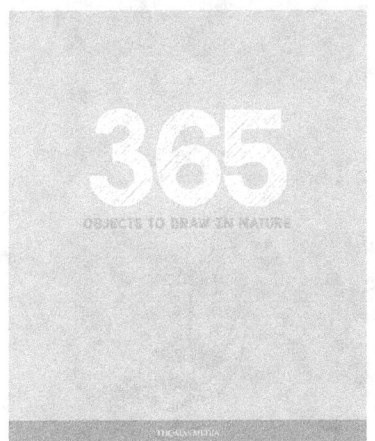
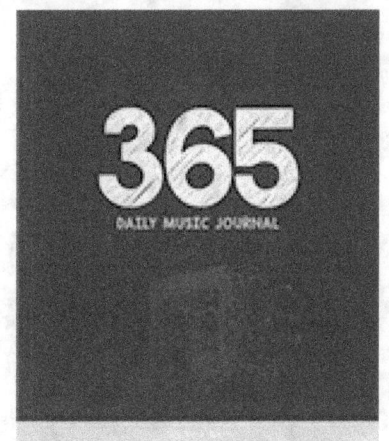
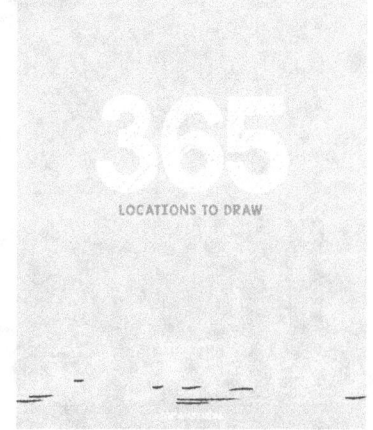

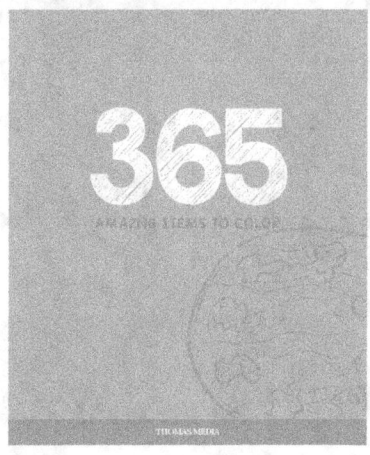

365 Creative Series

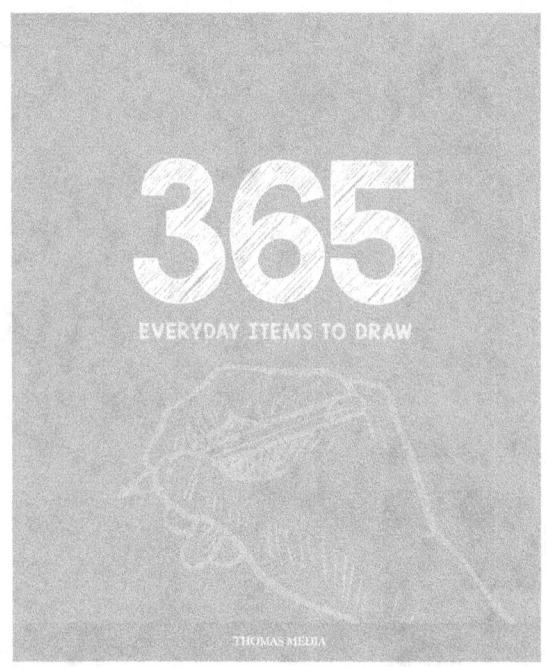
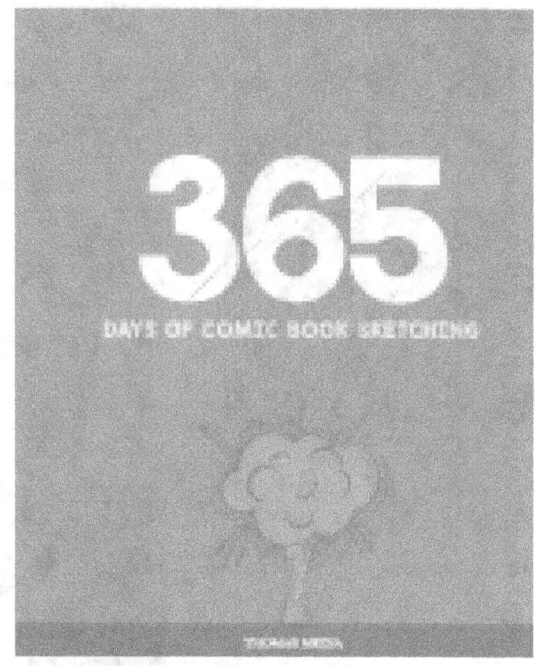
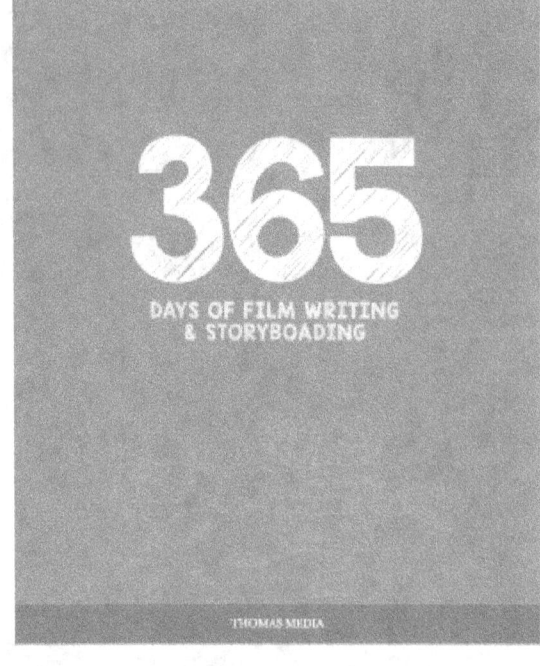
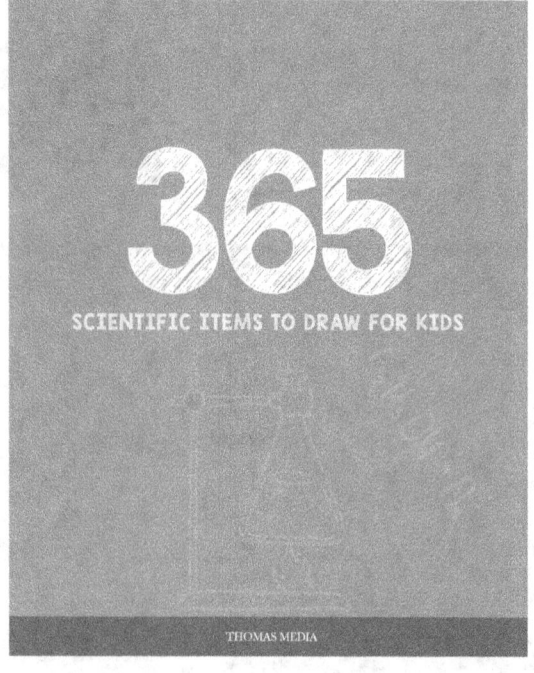

www.ingramcontent.com/pod-product-compliance
Lightning Source LLC
Chambersburg PA
CBHW080541220526
45466CB00010B/2989